THE WAR
WITHIN

THE WAR WITHIN

FLORINE PRICE

CITI OF BOOKS

CITIOFBOOKS, INC.
3736 Eubank NE Suite A1
Albuquerque, NM 87111-3579
www. citiofbooks. com

Hotline: 1 (877) 389-2759
Fax: 1 (505) 930-7244

Ordering Information:
Quantity sales. Special discounts are available on quantity purchases by corporations, associations, and others. For details, contact the publisher at the address above.

Printed in the United States of America.

| ISBN-13: | Softcover | 978-1-963209-68-6 |
| | eBook | 978-1-963209-69-3 |

Library of Congress Control Number: 2024903179

TABLE OF CONTENTS

DEDICATION

First, I dedicate this book back to God, who ministered to me while writing this book.

Secondly, I thank God for Al, my husband, who encouraged me through the process and teamed with Martina our daughter to edit this book.

Third, I thank God for my sisters (Doris and Ruby) and C Group sisters, who encouraged me, loved me unconditionally, and helped pray for me through this season.

Finally, I thank God for those who prayed for me as they anxiously awaited the completion of this book.

FOREWORD

All of us have a war within because we were born with a sinful nature. This sinful nature will be with us until the day we depart from this world. Because this is an ongoing war, we will constantly need God's word. God has placed people in the body of Christ with different gifts. One of the gifts that He has given us is teachers.

I am so grateful for the fivefold ministry: apostles, prophets, evangelists, pastors, and teachers. As a pastor, I am thankful for teachers. God's people will not come to maturity without teachers. I have known Minister Florine Price for several years now. Pastor Brenda and I have been blessed over the years by her presence. She came to this ministry and made herself available to serve the vision God gave us wherever help was needed. Minister Florine is a servant leader with a passionate heart to serve people. She has been so connected to Pastor Brenda and me, and she is also a part of our leadership here at the church. She is humble with her gift for teaching. Her faithfulness and dedication are noticeable.

This is not her first book, but I believe that this book will serve as a tool from God to help people win The War Within. Never has there been a time in our world like now, when we need anointed teachers to help fight this battle within. The pandemic has affected individuals in society tremendously. The mental battles have increased in all areas of our community. In all my life, I have never seen anything impact the world as COVID-19 has. However, I believe God has raised Minister Florine with these teachings as a tool to help equip people, especially to win the war within. I believe all of her battles and struggles have been a part of God's plan to help prepare her to write this material. She has been very transparent about her experiences and I believe this has allowed the Holy Spirit to help her write this book. The wisdom God has given her to share in this book will encourage, strengthen, and even bring breakthroughs in the lives of those who need it.

As you read this book, I believe you will sense her passion for and love of serving people. As she shares what God has given her, I believe it will be a tool that can be used in your daily walk with Christ. As you read each chapter, I hope you sense God's love unfold to you and even give you hope that you can win The War Within. This book contains the writings of a woman of God now in her mature adult years who wants to invite you into her life experiences. Throughout her life, she has seen and experienced God's grace for victory. So, enjoy partaking as you read her book.

Senior Pastor Ricky Harrell

Christ Worship Center Church, Hope Mills, NC

INTRODUCTION

The pandemic presented me with many mental challenges that I had never experienced before. When I began to seek God, He began to reveal truths about my life as never before. He began to pull back the layers of unresolved issues in my life that I had reopened. He opened up my soul, poured in His Word, and gave me spiritual insight into the war that was going on in my soul during this season of my life.

This is a small book, and in this book, with the help of the Holy Spirit, I will to the best of my ability, be transparent and share with you the mentally exhausting challenges that I experienced. Through my transparency, I pray that the Word of God will bring clarity to the mental challenges and/or the demonic influences that are operating in our lives.

Satan wants you and me to give up and quit God! Galatians 6:9 (KJV) says, "And let us not be weary in well doing: for in due season we shall reap if we faint not." He intends to prevent us from thriving in the way that God has proposed for us. During this season, I heard deep in my spirit Matthew 16:18 (NLT): "Now I say to you Peter (which means 'rock'), and upon this rock, I will build my church, and all the powers of hell will not conquer it." I experienced periods when I did not have peace or deep sleep. I was spiritually, mentally, and physically exhausted. I would go into a deep sleep for six to eight hours and still wake up exhausted. The continuous cycle repeated itself for months. However, my confession is that God is in control even during sleep deprivation.

There is an intense spiritual battle for my mind and my life. I felt oppressed with some signs of depression. But God allowed me to understand that Satan was trying to trick me back into the pit of deep depression from which I had previously been delivered.

The first book I wrote took me three years. This book, the Holy Spirit ministered to me in less than a year. There is a sense of urgency in my spirit. I will embark on this endeavor with the Holy Spirit guiding my thoughts and my words.

It is my desire to be transparent and share with you the mentally exhausting challenges and demonic attacks that are operating in my life and the truths that the Holy Spirit is revealing to me. Today I choose to put my name where it says Peter because I choose to believe that Satan will not win this battle (sift me). The Lord said, "Simon, Simon! Indeed, Satan has asked for you, that he may sift you as wheat. But I have prayed for you, that your faith should not fail; and when you have returned to Me, strengthen your brethren" (Luke 22:31–32 NKJV).

There were times when I felt that it would be easier to ask God to take me home. I thought about suicide, but previously God had told me that suicide was not an option for me. John 16:33 (KJV) says, "These things I have spoken unto you, that ye might have peace. In the world ye shall have tribulation: but be of good cheer; I have overcome the world."

In chapter eight, I will, with the help of the Holy spirit, describe how the spirit operates in our souls, and give scriptures to address specific strongholds. I meditate on the Word of God, calling on and recognizing the power and authority that is in the name of Jesus, and pleading the blood of Jesus over our spirits, souls, and bodies. I desire that we walk in our free-action status, for who the Son has set free is free indeed.

As you read this book, first hear the heart of God and His Word speaking to you. Isaiah 41:13 (NIV) says, "For I am the Lord your God who takes hold of your right hand and says to you, 'Do not fear; I will help you.'" Then hear my heart as the Holy Spirit unfolds The War Within me.

CHAPTER 1

THE STRUGGLE

We all have struggles in our walks with the Lord. From time to time, the issues of life become overwhelming. This includes the spiritual issues that come with being believers in Jesus Christ. Sometimes our souls become frustrated, our inner humans become tired, and we give up on God. Or we go from church to church looking for a better church. Second Timothy 4:3 (KJV) says, "For the time will come when they will not endure sound doctrine; but after their lust shall they heap to themselves teachers, having itchy ears;" This I hadn't done because I realized that if there was an issue, I needed to start with myself. Self-inventory I find to be good therapy. I had become busy with doing and no longer spent quality time with God. My plate was full, and on some days, the time with God was minimal to none. I had drifted away from my first love and the intimate times with Him. Intimacy with God to me is life (peace, joy, love, and righteousness in the Holy Ghost).

Being frustrated, I frustrated the people around me. I needed peace to be restored in my soul. Psalm 23:3 (KJV) says, "He restoreth my soul: He leadeth me in the path of righteousness for His name's sake." I needed a fresh touch from God. I knew deep within my soul that this would not happen without quality time with Him.

The Holy Spirit reminded me of Peter. He became frustrated with himself and walked away for a season. But when Jesus sent for him, he returned as a result of his obedience. Luke 22:32(KJV) recounts Jesus saying, "But I have prayed for thee, that thy faith fail not: and when thou art converted, strengthen thy brethren." How can I be an encouragement to someone else when I am limping? Satan desires to steal our relationship with God, our faith, and our ability to speak the Word of God into others' lives, but God is a restorer of the breach. He desires to restore us in Him and anoint us fresh. Then we, too, can fulfill our purposes.

Satan's ultimate goal is for us to fail, but Jesus intercedes for us. Luke 22:31–32 (KJV) says, "And the lord said, Simon, Simon, behold, Satan desires to have you, that he may sift you as wheat: But I have prayed for thee, that thy faith fails not: and when thou art converted, strengthen thy brethren." This is what he is trying to do to us. I must admit that since I moved to North Carolina, being "steadfastly unmovable always abounding in the work of the Lord" (1 Corinthians 15:58 KJV) has been difficult, but I keep pressing in, and I know that God will restore my complete faithfulness to Him. I believe in the restoration of my focus.

We talk about Peter going back to what he knew. But how many times have I gone back in my soul to the former things? The Holy Spirit tells me to do something; I continue what I am doing and forget. It is the next day when I remember or, even worse, the next week. It grieves my soul when I don't walk upright before Him, and I still fall short. Many times, have I neglected my relationship with God by not studying the Word.

I tend to digress, and there is no logical reason that I do not spend quality time in the Word. Without renewing my mind daily and as needed with the Word of God, I became spiritually anemic. Distractions and wayward thoughts have crowded out my peace, and have affected and infected my praise, worship, and ability to retain the Word as it was ministered.

God has reminded me that only what I do for Him will last. The praise team leader says to praise God. What do I do? My praise and worship are good. If I concentrate with my eyes closed in church, I connect with God, but if I keep my eyes open, my mind wanders. Yes, I struggle to stay focused. Remorse will cause guilt, shame, and condemnation to take root in our souls, but Peter was not reluctant to go when Jesus sent for him.

I needed restoration in my spirit, soul, and body. In my soul, I felt like a lost sheep at times. I was having hearing problems physically, and on some days, the noises in my ears and head were off the chart. To compound the issue, I needed cataract surgery on both eyes. Demon spirits do all they know to do to make you insecure. Hard of hearing and needing cataract surgery, my soul was in turmoil. When saved souls feel disconnected from God, there is a problem, and I am in trouble. It is the enemy's job to try to short-circuit the believer's relationship with God, but it is my responsibility to renew my mind daily with the Word of God. I found myself bingeing on television. Now I desire to turn off the frequency (the distractions) of Satan and to turn up the volume of God.

While in the struggle, I became insecure, and the insecurities manifested themselves in many ways. I had a bad temper. Sometimes, you just needed to look my way, and the attitude would be Whaaat? I think I just created a new word, but I pray that you will understand what I'm saying. I was on my way back to the pit of depression, and anger was unlocking the door, but I recognized the signs and symptoms.

Several years ago, I was depressed, and God allowed me to write a book titled Healing of the Soul. It took me three years to write it. I promised God and myself that I would not go back to that dark place. There were moments when I entertained the thought, and tears would come to my eyes because I knew the thoughts were not from God.

When a saved soul feels disconnected from God, there is a problem. John 10:4–5 (KJV) says, "And the sheep follow Him: for they know His voice. And a stranger will they not follow, but flee from him: for they know not the voice of strangers." The enemy's job is to try to short-circuit the believer's relationship with God. You can hear the signal, and it is scrambled, but it is the believer's responsibility to renew his or her mind daily with the Word of God. Frequently, I needed three or four doses of the Word of God daily. I think I am saying it right, but I must reread what I studied to be safe. Often, I meditate on the same scripture for days.

I began to reclaim my time with God. I felt like I was starting all over again. Starting over with Jesus is renewing and refreshing. I depended on the Holy Spirit to lead and guide me each day. Psalm 23:1–3 (KJV) says,

> The LORD is my Shepherd; I shall not want. He maketh me to lie down in green pastures: He leadeth me beside still waters. He restoreth my soul: He leadeth me in the paths of righteousness for His name's sake.

Our co-pastor told me that strongholds can come back when the root cause is not dealt with. Is this why people go back to addictive behaviors after rehabilitation? Better yet, is this why I can't get rid of bad attitudes that result in negative behaviors? I began to pray and asked God what the strongholds that I needed to let the Holy Spirit deal with were. I heard "abandonment" and "rejection."

My mother passed when I was one, and I always wondered why she transitioned. Her death was never discussed with me in detail. My father raised my two sisters and me. He was a nurturer and a provider. He never remarried. Yes, he had lady friends, but he told us he had three wives. I think he may have entertained remarriage, but it never happened. Occasionally, I wonder if things would have been different if my mother had been in my life. But God says in Isaiah 49:16 (NIV), "See, I have engraved you on the palms of My hands; your walls are ever before Me." What a promise, but deep in my soul, I still wonder. I realize that what-ifs can be dangerous. The phrase "what-if" has the potential to destroy your dreams and relationships and hinder the manifestation of the promises of God in your life. It can also destroy your confidence.

Rejection is the act of not accepting, believing, or considering something. According to the website Good Therapy, "In the mental health field, rejection most frequently refers to the feelings of shame, sadness, or grief people feel after a significant other ends a relationship." I will always remember when I was in the sixth grade, I went home with a classmate after school. We played for a couple of hours. Her brother rode me home on the back of his bike, and she rode her bike. The next day at recess, she announced that her mother said I was different because I did not have a mother—for real, on the playground in front of our classmates. Wow! The sixth grade was quite a year for me. Our teacher showed me two dimes with the faces outward. He asked me what happened between the two classmates. I did not take sides and told him what happened. In front of my peers, he announced that I was two-faced. I felt so ashamed that I could have slid under my desk. Mentally, the sixth grade was a rough year.

The Holy Spirit spoke to my heart that I am insecure in

relationships, but God has always been there for me. Psalm 27:10 (NLT) says, "Even if my father and mother abandoned me, the Lord will hold me close." I am seventy-two years old. I received Jesus as my personal Savior and the Lord of my life in 1986. I served as an assistant pastor for twenty-five years, and sometimes I struggle with who I am in Him. Forgive me, Jesus. My relationships (study of the Word, prayer, praise, and worship) are not as consistent as they once were. I have allowed my insecurities—the things that people say about me—to play with my mind, and the negative thoughts and fretting to control my thought life. Second Corinthians 10:4–5 (AMP) says,

> The weapons of our warfare are not physical [weapons of flesh and blood]. Our weapons are divinely powerful for the destruction of fortresses. We are destroying sophisticated arguments and every exalted and proud thing that sets itself up against the [true] knowledge of God, and we are taking every thought and purpose captive to the obedience of Christ.

Someone might wonder if God called me. My answer is yes! He called me to preach and teach, but I allowed my soul to go to a dry place by not communing with God consistently. Psalm 37:7 (NLT) says, "Be still in the presence of the LORD, and wait patiently for Him to act." This I do not do well, but I am learning not to be a fixer. Instead, I am learning to make a conscious decision to make my request known to God and let Him fix it.

My husband tells me that I fret too much and allow things to bother me. I struggle with staying in the peace of God, and the struggle breaks my spiritual and physical rest. As we read in Philippians 4:7 (KJV), "And the peace of God, which passeth all understanding, shall keep your hearts and minds through Christ Jesus."

For a season, it appeared in my mind that I made bad decisions repeatedly, and at times I would get tired of making decisions. I pray about matters, but when you are tired in your inner man, you fret before and after you have acted. You say I am double-minded. Maybe but I am truthful. James 1:2–4 (NIV) says,

> Consider it pure joy, my brothers and sisters, whenever you face trials of many kinds, because you know that the testing of your faith produces perseverance. Let perseverance finish its work so that you may be mature and complete, not lacking anything.

I would love to live worry-free. The Holy Spirit continues to remind me to cast my cares on Him because He cares for me. Psalm 55:22 (KJV) reads, "Cast your burden upon the LORD, and He shall sustain thee: He shall never suffer the righteous to be moved."

Three winters ago, Al, my husband, fell down the stairs, and for most of that year, I took on most of the responsibilities. Mentally, it was overwhelming for me, but the Holy Spirit was navigating me through this new season of life called added responsibility. Some days, Al could barely walk. He does what I call furniture walking. He would bend his knees to take the pressure off his back. He started getting epidurals, and they helped his back, but he still had headaches. Frequently, I would think to myself, God, it is You and me. I felt like I did not want to do life anymore for a few weeks, but I never said it to him. He expressed that he was concerned about me, but with the help of the Holy Spirit, He picked me up. Yes, life was much but God is greater than any struggle I could face. I tear up as I think about this season of our lives, but God is taking me through this valley.

I would wake up mentally exhausted in the mornings

because day-to-day affairs played in my head all night. Did I mention that there are noises in my head that compound the issue? The medical name is tinnitus. The day-to-day affairs plus the noises are unbearable. But each day God woke me up, and the Holy Spirit took over from there. My days were not easy, and some days, the noises and the recorded messages of the things that I needed to accomplish were overpowering. One day I felt like telling my pastor that I wanted to quit Follow Up. I told the elder what I was thinking, and she said, "If you quit, Satan will have a good time in your head."

I became more isolated in my mind and protective of my thoughts. I did not talk because I did not want to say the wrong thing and be judged. But God keeps on keeping me. My thoughts were intense, and I wanted to scream. One day Al was playing with me. He had the remote, and I wanted it. When he gave it to me, I snatched it out of his hand so hard that the back came off, and the batteries were on the floor. I thought to myself, Am I losing my mind? Some people talked to me, but they did not offer to pray with me. Some said that they were praying for me. Or did they pray about me?

Then came COVID (I think). Time and months run together, but things have been intertwined in my mind for the last two-plus years. Al tries to help me remember, but I don't. It irritates me when he says, "Don't you remember?" If I remembered, I would not be trying to recall my thoughts. It is a struggle on most days to have clarity of thought, but I consciously ask the Holy Spirit to bring things to my remembrance and to keep my mind.

Now my dilemma is, do I stay home, or do I go back to church? God helped me to make my way back to church. I struggled in my mind to go back to church, and my insecurities came with me. But I am not a runner. I look to God for Him to fix me in place. I have a problem with people being in my space without a mask. Medically speaking, I am immune compromised, but I know that God is a protector. Second Timothy 1:7 (KJV) says, "For God has not given us the spirit of fear; but of power, and love, and a sound mind."

Focus Scripture: Psalm 27:10 (NLT): "Even if my father and mother abandon me, the LORD will hold me close."

CHAPTER 2

CASTING DOWN IMAGINATIONS

Since I am to cast down imaginations and pull down strongholds, I understand that I will engage in spiritual warfare. The Word must be spoken, and I must dress consistently for the battle. I must also be skilled in using the ammunition that God has given me.

I invite you to study hall with me. The Word of God is never boring. Let's lock into the battle plan for casting down imaginations. Imagination is "the act or power of forming a mental image of something not present to the senses or never before perceived in reality." Second Corinthians 10:5 (KJV) says, "Casting down imaginations, and every high thing that exalteth itself against the knowledge of God and bringing into captivity every thought to the obedience of Christ." My husband told me that "a good defense is a strong offense." Never allow your time with God to have gaps in it. This I did not do well for a season. First Thessalonians 5:16–18 (NKJV) reads, "Rejoice always, pray without ceasing, in everything give thanks; for this is the will of God in Christ Jesus for you."

The Word says we must dress for the battle. When we

dress, we must have confidence in the armor of God. It is our responsibility to keep each piece tightened with the Word. Our weapons are the Word of God, the name of Jesus, the precious Blood of Jesus, prayer, praise, and worship. Also, we must activate our faith and confidence in our weapons.

Now we know that we are to dress for spiritual warfare and have weapons. The Word of God tells us to cast down imaginations and to pull down strongholds. We are to cast down thoughts that do not line up with the Word of God and replace them with the Word of God. I reviewed several translations of scripture until I understood what God was saying to me. A better way to explain what I am saying is that I must pray and renew my mind daily with the Word of God until I have understanding and the peace of God in my heart. There is a scripture for every battle. For example, if you are sick, remember that by Jesus' stripes, you are healed. If you are weary, consider casting your cares on Him because He cares for you. The wayward thoughts will continue to torment us and manifest themselves until we become dependent on God. Once there is peace, the wayward thoughts will cease to exist, and the thoughts will line up with the Word of God. The images and false beliefs that Satan has entrenched in our brains must be cast down with the Word. As we read in 2 Corinthians 10:4–5 (NIV),

> The weapons we fight with are not weapons of this world. On the contrary, they have the divine power to demolish strongholds. We demolish arguments and every pretension that sets itself up against the knowledge of God, and we take captive every thought to make it obedient to Christ.

I needed to allow the Holy Spirit to sharpen my weapons and tighten my armor.

There was a fortress of strongholds in my soul. A fortress is a reinforced structure, often surrounding and protecting a town. These strongholds had set up residence in my soul. I'm seventy-three years old and God is still delivering me from old emotional wounds. Those wounds were the result of the lies of the enemy. It was a lie that Satan had established in my head, and I embraced it. A fortress is a fortified place where the lies affected and infected my attitude, emotions, and behaviors. The lies manifested themselves through a characteristic that I will call insecurities. The devil plants insecurities to help embellish or promote false beliefs. The insecurities open the soul to deceptions, and I became vulnerable to the lies and trickery of the enemy that grew strongholds. There were sixty years of roots intertwined in my soul. The turmoil in my soul was a playground for the enemy to work and wreak havoc in my life. Wow! Sixty years later, my soul was still filled with the deceptive lies of Satan.

The insecurities are designed to manipulate a person into following Satan and thus block the blessings that God has purposed for a person's life. His ultimate goal is to keep you entangled in the web of his craftiness. Galatians 5:1 (KJV) says, "Stand fast therefore in the liberty wherewith Christ hath made us free, and be not entangled again with the yoke of bondage." The manipulations cause us to live in the bondage of slavery. This is where realization set in. I have confessed that Jesus is the Lord of my life, but I was in bondage to the strongholds of Satan. He is looking for an opening to destroy us, twist our purposes, and magnify himself. Remember, this is the reason that he was kicked out of heaven. He wanted to exalt himself above his creator (God). First Peter 5:8 (KJV) says, "Be sober, be vigilant, because your adversary the devil, as a roaring lion, walketh about, seeking whom he may devour."

God gives us instructions and warnings in His Word: be sober and vigilant because your enemy prowls, seeking whom he may devour. When I received the lie, I was twelve and not saved. I came to Jesus with all my brokenness and shame. He loves me regardless of what is going on in my head.

Back to the battle (the strongholds). When we fight, our armor and weapons have the power to demolish the manipulations of the enemy. Every believer can have the mind of Christ. As we read in Romans 12:2 (KJV), "And be not conformed to this world: but be ye transformed by the renewing of your mind, that ye may prove what is that good, and acceptable, and perfect, will of God."

The Word says to demolish, to pull down or knock down, to overwhelmingly defeat the strongholds and take captive (imprison or confine) every thought to the obedience of Christ. Satan will have you thinking right is wrong and wrong is right. Isaiah 5:20 (NIV) says, "Woe to those who call evil good and good evil." My mind was in turmoil. My mind was in constant motion. Sometimes the turmoil was so intense that I did not think straight. My responses and actions were not appropriate. The stronghold intends to do what the word says. To build strongholds is to build fortified areas in our souls. The goal is to pack our souls with lies or take the truth and twist it. The scripture uses the word prowl. The meaning of the word prowl is "to move about or wander stealthily in or as if in search of prey." The purpose is to kill, steal, and destroy relationships with God, ourselves, and others. John 10:10 (KJV) says, "The thief cometh not, but for to steal, and to kill, and to destroy: I come that they might have life and that they might have it more abundantly."

The Holy Spirit is still uncluttering my soul. What kind of love is this? I know that God says that His love is unconditional and that He is long-suffering. The Holy Spirit is guiding me and the Word of God is demolishing the influences of the strongholds that had rooted and grounded themselves in my soul. Second Corinthians 10:4 (KJV) says, "(For the weapons of our warfare are not carnal, but mighty through God to the pulling down of strongholds)." I believe that the Holy Spirit is sharpening my weapons.

What plan does God have for our lives? Jeremiah 29:11 (NIV) says, "'For I know the plans I have for you,' declares the LORD, 'plans to prosper you and not to harm you, plans to give you hope and a future.'" God has planted dreams in my heart that have not come to fruition yet. But I believe in the work that He has started in me. He will complete it. Philippians 1:6 (KJV) says, "Being confident of this very thing, that He which hath begun a good work in you will perform it until the day of Jesus Christ." The negative thinking was often against me. Satan will convince you that you are not intelligent, skilled, or educated enough to do what God has proposed for you to do. But God will take our weaknesses and turn them into strengths for His glory.

My emotions were anger, bitterness, and resentment. These emotions were designed to block the plan and purpose that God has for my life. For example, if I despise looking at you, and you look at me, something might be said. The mean spirit that had embedded itself in my soul helped me to justify my negative response or reaction. However, this spirit needed to be uprooted and demolished with the Word of God and a Christian mental health counselor. If Satan can block the anointing of God on your life, he can and will block your purpose. We must stand on the Word of God.

To be successful in the battle, we must dress for the war. Ephesians 6:12–18 (NIV) says,

For our struggle is not against flesh and blood, but against the rulers, against the authorities, against the powers of this dark world, and the spiritual forces of evil in the heavenly realms. Therefore, put on the whole armor of God, so that when the evil day comes, you may stand your ground, after you have done everything to stand. Stand firm then, with the belt of truth buckled around your waist, with the breastplate of righteousness in place, and with your feet fitted with the readiness that comes from the gospel of peace. In addition to all of this, take up the shield of faith, with which you can extinguish all the flaming arrows of the evil one. Take the helmet of salvation and the sword of the Spirit, which is the Word of God. And pray in the Spirit on all occasions with all kinds of prayers and requests. With this in mind, be alert and always keep on praying for all the Lord's people.

We must consistently tighten our armor with the Word of God. Satan is looking for a crack to entangle us again. God has given us the required ammunition (the Word) for every battle so that we might be victorious. Remember when Satan tried to tempt Jesus? His response was, "It is written." This must be our response also. According to Matthew 4:4 (NJKV), But He answered and said, "It is written, 'Man shall not live by bread alone, but by every word that proceeds from the mouth of God.'" We are overcomers and more than conquerors through Christ Jesus, who strengthens us. The Holy Spirit is guiding us. We are casting down imaginations, pulling down strongholds, and we are ready to run the race with endurance. Hebrews 12:1–2 (NIV) says,

Let us throw off everything that hinders and the sin that so easily entangles. And let us run with perseverance the race marked out for us, fixing our eyes on Jesus, the pioneer, and perfector of faith. For the joy set before Him, He endured the cross, scorning its shame, and sat down at the right hand of the throne of God.

I hope you enjoyed the study hall and maybe the Holy Spirit will invite us to another one in the future.

Focus Scripture: Philippians 4:8 (NIV): "Finally,

brothers and sisters, whatever is true, whatever is noble, whatever is right, whatever is pure, whatever is lovely, whatever is admirable, if anything is excellent or praiseworthy—think about such things."

CHAPTER 3

TOXINS WITHIN

There are a few terms that I will be using to bring clarity to what I'm saying and to keep the terms straight in my mind. I would like to define them for us.

Toxin: "an antigenic poison or venom of plant origin, especially one produced by or derived from microorganisms and causing disease when present at low concentrations in the body."

A poison is "a substance which, when taken into the stomach, mixed with the blood or applied to the skin or flesh, proves fatal or deleterious by action not mechanical; venom. The more active and virulent poisons destroy life in a short time: others are slow in theory operation, others produce inflammation without proving fatal. In the application, much depends on quantity."

Demonic oppression is when a demon is temporarily victorious over a Christian, successfully tempting a Christian to sin and hindering his ability to serve God with a strong testimony. If a Christian continues to allow demonic oppression in his/her life, the oppression can increase to the point that the demon has a very strong influence over the Christian's thoughts, behaviors, and spirituality. Christians who allow continuing sin open themselves up for greater and greater oppression. Confession and repentance of sin are necessary to restore fellowship with God, who can break the power of the demonic influence. The apostle John gives us great encouragement in this area; "We know that anyone born of God does not continue in sin; the one who was born of God keeps him safe, and the evil one cannot harm him" (1 John 5:18).

A spiritual toxin can be bitterness, anger, and resentment that will eventually turn into unforgiveness. Unforgiveness is poison to the soul. These toxins can cause physical and mental stress, which can lead to physical and mental illness. Romans 7:2–23 (NIV) says, "So I find this law at work: Although I want to do good, evil is right there with me. For in my inner being, I delight in God's law, but I see another law at work in me, waging war against the law of my mind, and making me a prisoner of the law of sin at work in me." No, I'm not a psychiatrist or a psychologist, but I'm sharing what God has revealed to me through His Word and my life experiences.

The Holy Spirit dwells in each believer, and we can be oppressed and depressed by demonic spirits. However, the believer who truly confesses Jesus as the Lord of his or her life cannot be possessed by a demon. Ephesians 1:13–14 (NLT) says,

> And now you Gentiles have also heard the truth, the Good news that God saves you. And when you believed in Christ, He identified you as His own by giving you the Holy Spirit, whom He promised long ago. The Spirit is God's guarantee that He will give us the inheritance He promised and that He purchased us to be His people.

As we read in Romans 7:21–23 (NKJV), "I find then a law, that evil is present with me, the one who wills to do good. For I delight in the law of God according to the inward man. But I see another law in my members, warring against the law of my mind, and bringing me into captivity to the law of sin which is in my members." Bitterness, anger resentment, and anxiety can cause physical and mental stress. This can lead to illness or death.

These toxins had embedded themselves in my mind to the point that I did not think clearly. But the Word says, in 2 Timothy 1:7 (KJV), "For God has not given us the spirit of fear; but of power, and love, and a sound mind." The influences had grown and were fertilized by old emotional wounds.

Before receiving Christian mental health counseling, a person could make a negative comment to me, and it would trigger my anger. I did and said things that were not kind. The words or actions would be compounded by frustration. The frustration would cause anxiety. Philippians 4:6–7 (NKJV) says, "Be anxious for nothing, but in everything by prayer and supplication, with thanksgiving, let your request be made known to God; and the peace which surpasses all understanding, will guard your hearts and minds through Christ Jesus." For a season, I did not ask the Holy Spirit to keep my mind.

Why was I so anxious? I'm so glad you asked. Anxiety is produced by uncertainty. I would second-guess myself and fear would manifest itself. When double-mindedness came into play, my thoughts were very unstable. James 1:8 (KJV) says, "A double-minded man is unstable in all of his ways." This was me. Pastor Brenda had me journal daily about my struggles and accomplishments. I had many battles, and one of the major characteristics was an unstable thought life. My mind was always busy. There was a period when I did not think rationally. She reinforced that I should greet the Holy Spirit each morning and bind the mind of Christ to my mind. Then I should confess that I have the mind of Christ. I will speak positive words and meditate on the Word of God. I began to think if it was good for morning prayer, it had to be equally as effective for my night prayer. Even in my sleep, my mind was occupied with the events of tomorrow. For months I did not sleep well, even though 1 Peter 5:7 (AMP) says to cast "all your cares [all your anxieties, all your worries, and all your concerns, once and for all] on Him, for He cares about you [with deepest affection, and watches over you carefully]." What about all that did I not understand?

Mental stress can lead to heart attack, stroke, high blood pressure, and other heart-related issues; doctors tell us these can lead to death. A cardiologist in Denver once told me that I could deal with the stress in my life, or it would deal with me. Stress is a spiritual toxin and a physical diagnosis. Yes, it can kill you naturally and poison you spiritually. Second Timothy 1:7 (KJV) says, "For God hath not given us a spirit of fear; but of power, and love, and a sound mind." I think to myself, how many dreams did I abort because I was anxious about things? Did I grieve the Holy Spirit? Forgive me, God, because I think I did. Some toxins had turned into poison in my soul. Psalm 139:23–24 (NIV) says, "Search me, God, and know my heart; test me and know my anxious thoughts. See if there is any offensive way in me, and lead me in the way everlasting." I had never asked the Holy Spirit to govern my thought life. I have asked the Holy Spirit to search for and reveal to me doors, portals, and cracks that were open for demonic influences to operate in my soul (my life).

We have the ability through Jesus Christ to demolish strongholds. 2 Corinthians 10:3–6 (KJV) says,

For though we walk in the flesh, we do not war after the flesh: (For the weapons of our warfare are not carnal, but mighty through God to the pulling down of strongholds;)

Casting down imaginations, and every high thing that exalteth itself against the knowledge of God, and bringing into captivity every thought to the obedience of Christ. And having in readiness to revenge all disobedience, when your obedience is fulfilled.

I would pray and ask God to deliver me, but I did not consistently fill the voided spaces with the Word of God. Lately, my time with God has been more consistent. Regardless of what is going on in my life, I asked God to heal my brain, but what did I fill it with? My prayer is that God will cleanse me, heal me in spirit, soul, and body, and fill me afresh. As we read in Psalm 51:10 (KJV), "Create in me a clean heart, O God, and renew a right spirit within me." Satan had studied my insecurities and my shortcomings to the point that I felt inadequate, but I can do all things through Christ Jesus, who strengthens me. Some of my dreams never came to fruition because I had learned to talk myself out of things. For example, I was going to college to be a registered nurse. I got a C in microbiology because I had issues with being taught that humans came from amoebas. I allowed the devil to trick me out of the dream of being a registered nurse. It is sad but true.

I had gone around the mountain of bitterness, anger, resentment, and frustration too many times to the point that the toxins had affected my relationship with God, myself, and others. I concluded that the toxins had oppressed and depressed me long enough. Pastor Brenda shared with me that the root cause of the problem had to be dealt with. Christian counseling has made a difference in my life. Learning to deal with the negative thoughts has been a plus.

She also addressed the old emotional wounds that had become deeply rooted in my soul. Pastor Brenda explained that the roots would lay dormant for some time and then resurface. Each time I would think about it, the spirit would become more aggressive to the point that my words and actions would spiritually wound others. I would repent before God, and He would send me to ask that person to forgive me. This season lasted for three or more years. I have been in counseling since the middle of November 2021, and there is peace in my soul that surpasses all my understanding. Philippians 4:6–7 (NLT) says, "Don't worry about anything; instead, pray about everything. Tell God what you need and thank Him for all He has done. Then you will experience God's peace, which exceeds anything we can understand. His peace will guard your hearts and minds as you live in Christ Jesus." Sometimes torment tries to return, but I speak aloud to the spirits and tell them (bitterness, anger, resentment, and unforgiveness) that they can't return to me again in the name of Jesus. I'm in a covenant relationship with God and I will not open the door for the enemy to return by allowing toxins to reenter my soul. John 8:36 (NIV) says, "So if the Son sets you free, you will be free indeed." Now I deliberately ask the Holy Spirit to control my mind, guard my thoughts, and every imagination, and guard my mouth.

Focus Scripture: Psalm 139:23–24 (NIV): "Search me, O God, and know my heart; test me and know my anxious thoughts. See if there is any offensive way in me, and lead me in the way everlasting."

CHAPTER 4

THE NOISES

I have been praying about sharing this chapter for a few months. Did I want to share the most intimate inward parts of my soul? There are noises in my head and negative energy that surrounds it periodically. By the end of this chapter, my prayer is to be free of both. I do not have the words to articulate what I am thinking, but I am confident that the Holy Spirit will navigate me through this chapter as He has the others. I stand on the Word of God, and I take my position by faith, knowing that God will do what He says He will do. Psalm 103:2–4 (NKJV) says, "Bless the LORD, O my soul, And forget not all of His benefits: Who forgives all your iniquities, Who heals all your diseases, Who redeems your life from destruction, Who crowns you with loving kindness and tender mercies."

The noises in my head/ears are overpowering at times, and there seems to be negative energy around my head when the noises are the loudest. It feels like electrical energy coming off my scalp. Before I go further, Pastor Brenda encouraged me to declare that by Jesus' stripes, I am healed of tinnitus and to bind the mind of Christ to my mind. I declare by the Blood of Jesus I am delivered from the negative energy. The energy is less intense and is not persistent. I thank God for the healing and deliverance. I continue to pray about the noises and the energy. I believe by faith they will be gone completely. My proclamation is I am set free. John 8:36 (NIV) says, "So if the Son sets you free, you will be free indeed." My heart desires to walk in my free indeed status.

Also, I pray and cover Al, myself, and those whom I come in contact with and declare that there will be no transfer of spirits.

I would like to focus on the noises first. I think that medical diagnosis can be an indicator that there might be demonic influences operating in our lives—the lives of believers. We can be oppressed or depressed but not possessed. As we read in Ephesians 1:13–14 (NKJV), "In Him you also trusted, after you heard the word of truth, the gospel of salvation; in whom also, having believed, you were sealed with the Holy Spirit of promise, who[a] is the [b]guarantee of our inheritance until the redemption purchased possession, to the praise of His glory."

During one of my sessions with Pastor Brenda, she told me to find the scripture in Philippians that teaches me how to think. Let me/us focus on how to think. Philippians 4:8 (NIV) says, "Finally brothers and sisters, whatever is true, whatever is noble, whatever is right, whatever is pure, whatever is lovely, whatever is admirable—if anything is excellent or praiseworthy—think about such things." To keep my mind clear from the noises of the enemy, focusing on and filling my mind with the Word of God is a must. When I'm not near a Bible, I speak the Word. That's right; I have my cell phone, and I can pull Word up. This allows the Word of God, the name of Jesus, and the precious shed Blood of Jesus to deliver me from the noises. Deliver me from all evil. As it says in Matthew 6:13 (KJV), "But deliver us from the evil: For thine is the kingdom, and the power, and the glory, forever. Amen." It is evil because torment is not from God. Even though there are noises, I can still hear the voice of the Holy Spirit. I know it is Him because He speaks the Word of God. He speaks life and life more abundantly.

The Word says speak to the mountain and deliverance comes from speaking the Word of God. In Matthew 17:20 (NIV), He replied, "Because you have so little faith. Truly I tell you, if you have faith as a mustard seed, you can say to this mountain, 'Move from here to there,' and it will move. Nothing will be impossible for you." Twice I have been diagnosed with cancer and twice He has healed me. I know Him to be a healer. Daily I speak the Word to the noises (tinnitus). By Jesus' stripes, my mental health is sound. I confess that I have the mind of Christ. The Blood of Jesus has delivered us from all evil and cleanses us from all unrighteousness (toxins within). First John 1:9 (KJV) says, "If we confess our sins, He is faithful and just to forgive our sins and to cleanse us from all unrighteousness." Satan uses our struggles against us. We must decide to use the Word of God against him. Psalm 37:23–24 (NLT) says, "The LORD directs the steps of the godly. He delights in every detail of their lives. Though they stumble, they will never fall, the LORD holds them by the hand." The purpose of the spirit torment is to steal our peace and rest. This weapon of the enemy must go in the name of Jesus. Isaiah 54:17 (KJV) says, "No weapon formed against thee shall prosper."

I would like to take a sidebar here and talk to two special groups of people. God loves us and He heals our pain.

I am retired from the Army with twenty years of service, and I would like to say that the noises in your ears are probably from the firing of weapons. Please take care of yourselves and go to see the doctor. Take care of yourself and do what you can to alleviate the noise. You were serving our country and be proud of that. Freedom is not free and often time leaves us with residual effects from our military occupation specialty. Know that Jesus loves you and you speak the Word. John 3:16 (KJV) says, "For God so loved the world, that He gave His only begotten Son, that whosoever believeth in Him should not perish, but have everlasting life." Please don't commit suicide. God loves us unconditionally, and by Jesus' stripes, we are healed.

To my battered sisters and brothers, the noises in your ears/head may be from years of physical abuse. Please take care of yourselves and get Christian counseling. You did nothing wrong. God loves us and we did not deserve those beatings. You should have no guilt, no shame, and no condemnation. It does not matter what people say. You were made in God's image, and He says that we are skillfully and wonderfully made by Him. Remember to focus on the fact that God loves you. Hold your head up high and pull your shoulders back for you are the apple of His eye. Call out to Him. 1 Peter 5:7 (KJV) says, "Casting all your care on Him; for He careth or you." He is waiting for you, and He will answer you. He hears your silent cries and sees your tears. Psalm 56:8 (AMP) says, "You have taken account of my wanderings; Put my tears in Your bottle. Are they not recorded in Your book?" He knows our pain. He knows our shame. Give it all to Him. I do not have the words to articulate how much He cares for you. My eyes are tearing as the Holy Spirit ministers these words into my spirit. He is not ignorant of the devices that Satan uses to keep us from reaching our full potential and living peaceful lives. He is the God of restoration. God loves us and desires to heal and deliver us from the pit of turmoil (the noises). Please, if you are on medication, do not stop taking your medication until you are released by the prescribing person. Before ending this sidebar, I would like to make sure there is no misunderstanding. Al (my husband) had nothing to do with this abuse. He has always been concerned about my welfare. This is the end of the sidebar.

As believers, we can open doors for the enemy to operate in

our lives. These are examples of the ways that I think I opened the door of my soul to the enemy.

- Disobedience to God.
- Unwillingness to forgive.
- Harboring toxins (bitterness, anger, resentment, and unforgiveness) in my soul and my heart. These are not from God, but I embraced them when I refused to forgive and let go. I made a conscious decision to be disobedient.

These are the ways that I think demonic influences were manifested in my life.

- A feeling of heaviness—oppression and depression.
- Sickness with no cause.
- Low self-esteem and comparing myself to others, even though God says that we are beautifully and wonderfully made.
- Using mind-altering drugs. I went to the hospital for a procedure, and I do not recall praying over the medication. Let me share an experience with you. I always let the anesthesiologist know that I can take half of a Tylenol with codeine and sleep for twenty-four hours. I think the person heard me, but the person gave me fentanyl for my body weight. I was in the recovery room. I could hear Al and the nurse, and they could hear me but I felt trapped and could not come out. That was a frightening feeling for me, I could entertain a conversation, but I could not see anyone. The nurse gave me something. Within a minute or so I could see.

Second is the spirit which I call negative energy. Do I have neurological problems? I don't know. But I do know that it is not from God. He would not give me a husband who requires my assistance and then send tormenting spirits to oppress and depress me.

Pastor Harrell told me one Sunday during the altar call that Satan was trying to steal the word that God had put in my spirit.

Pastor Brenda told me to bind the mind of Christ to my mind. To bind means to tie together or confine with a cord or anything flexible. Matthew 18:18 (KJV) says, "Verily I say unto you, Whatsoever ye shall bind on earth shall be bound in heaven: and whatsoever ye shall loose on earth shall be loosed in heaven." I chose to speak positively and to speak the Word. The Word says I have the mind of Christ. I might not act like it, but First Corinthians 2:16 (KJV) says, "For who hath the mind of the Lord, that He may instruct him? But we have the mind of Christ." Therefore, the Holy Spirit desires to bring balance to my mind, thoughts, and imagination and to stop the noises in my head. Jesus does not have noises in His head. These noises were sent to terrorize me, but I intend to put an end to being the victim by speaking the Word of God, pleading the Blood of Jesus over my mind, and calling on the name of Jesus. Psalm 34:17 (NIV) says, "The righteous cry out, and the LORD hears them; He delivers them from all their troubles." We plead the Blood of Jesus. But what do we want His Blood to do? If it is healing, say healing; if it is deliverance say so; if protection, say so; if finances, say so. Whatever it is, say so. He allowed Himself to be hung on the cross so that we might have life and have it more abundantly. John 10:10 (KJV) reads, "The thief cometh not, but to steal, and to kill, and to destroy: I come that they might have life and that they might have it more abundantly." I plead the Blood of Jesus and I am specific over my head (my hair, scalp, skull, brain, synapses, neurons, transmitters, and the cochlea and ossicles (the sound components inside of my ears). I plead over my ears, all around my ears, including the bones behind my ears, and over every component in my ears. I name the parts of the ear that I remember (the cochlea, the hair-like projections, the ear drum, and every moveable and immovable part). Yes, God, and cover my eyes and control my mouth. I am deliberate and focused. Revelation 12:11 (KJV) leads me in warfare: "And they overcame him (Satan) by the blood of the Lamb (Jesus), and the word of their testimony." I believe that Jesus is our High Priest and our advocate and that He presents our petitions to the Father for us. We read in 1 John 2:1 (KJV) that "If any man sin, we have an advocate with the Father, Jesus Christ the righteous."

I confess Jesus as Lord of my life and in the name of Jesus I focus and consciously release the authority, and protection in the spirit and natural realms. I thank God for clarity and remembrance.

The Word of God decrees that we are new creatures in Christ Jesus. We must speak by faith that sickness or disease can't thrive in our bodies. There is no sickness in the DNA of Jesus. First John 4:17(b) (KJV) says, "Because as He is, so are we in this world." Our lives are hidden with Christ Jesus in God. As Jesus is in health, so are we in this world. We can speak life and health over our physical, spiritual, emotional, and mental well-being in the mighty name of Jesus Christ and expect healing. "As He is, so are we in this world!" We partake in communion. The bread represents His body, and the wine represents His blood. By Jesus's stripes, we are healed. We read this in 1 Peter 2:24–25 (NKJV).

> Who Himself bore our sins in His own body on the tree, that we, having died to sins, might live for righteousness— by whose stripes ye were healed. For you were like sheep going astray, but are now returned unto the Shepherd and Overseer of your souls.

Jesus' blood has eradicated the tormenting noises, mental health challenges, and all malfunctioning parts of my brain, and ears.

In Jesus, I'm whole and complete. Shalom nothing is missing and nothing is broken. He delivered us from all tormenting spirits. This I believe and receive by faith in the finished works of Jesus Christ.

I have learned to speak the Word of God to myself and over myself, whether it is for a medical diagnosis or a demonic influence. What does the report of the Lord say? Whose report will we make a conscious decision to believe and receive? We must choose to believe the report of the Lord. By His stripes, we are healed in spirit, soul, and body. Psalm 103:2–3 (KJV) says, "Bless the LORD, O my soul, and forget not all His benefits: Who forgiveth all thine iniquities; who healeth all thy diseases." I bind the Word of God to my mind in the name of Jesus.

As we read in 1 John 3:8 (KJV), "For this purpose the Son of God was manifested, that He might destroy the works of the devil." This tells me that the noises and the toxins have been destroyed, but only by faith in the completed works of Jesus. I must continue to speak and believe the Word of God. Hebrews 12:24 (AMP) says, "And to Jesus, the Mediator of a new covenant [uniting God and man], and to the sprinkled blood, which speaks [of mercy], a better and nobler and more gracious message than the blood of Abel [which cried out for vengeance]."

Lately, when I have spoken to the noises, I open the front and/or back door for the enemy to leave me and exit my home. Yes, you must tell it to leave; tell it to go or it will hang out and reinvent itself and return. Yes, I have been outside before day asking God to sweep me and fill me afresh with His Holy Spirit.

This morning, I opened the window in the storm door and commanded the evil spirit to leave Al and myself, everything that pertains to us, and our home in the name of Jesus. There is a spirit of oppression and depression that lingers in our home.

I realized that I needed to address it. Al now shows signs and symptoms of depression. Recently he shared with me what was going on in his head. Then he said to me that it is like when you were depressed. This spoke volumes to me because I remember how I felt.

Al rebuked me because he thought I was back outside at four in the morning. He was afraid someone might harm me. Fear is not welcome, nor can it live in our hearts or our homes. I can say with a pure heart to be absent from this body is to be present with the Lord. In my flesh, I have many imperfections, but Jesus is my personal Savior and the Lord of my life.

Focus scripture: Revelation 12:11 (KJV): "And they overcame him (Satan) by the blood of the Lamb (Jesus), and the Word of their testimony."

CHAPTER 5

SELF-FORGIVENESS

Self-forgiveness has been a work in progress in my life for years. I have been focusing on allowing the Holy Spirit to separate who I am from my past mistakes and/or the poor choices I have made and give me clarity on who I am in this season of my life. We seek and ask others to forgive us, and we should. Mark 11:25 (KJV) says, "And when we stand praying, forgive, if ye have ought against any: that your Father also which is in heaven may forgive you your trespasses." Frequently, I struggle to forgive and release those who did me wrong. I call it "did me dirt." I had a Bible teacher who taught us to pray this: "By an act of my faith I release my will to forgive." But I have learned that there is nothing wrong with my faith in God or the Word. The real issue is my will. Am I truly willing to forgive to the point that the thought that triggers the unforgiveness will not resurface?

Let us take self-forgiveness to the point that we declare that we will forgive ourselves. Can I not release my faith to forgive myself also? Do I not choose to be free? I propose to you that it's my choice. The will is my emotions and attitudes about situations or the sins that I have committed. The desire to forgive myself for the many blunders that I have made in life is real. But the same issues keep coming up. Philippians 4:7 (AMP) says, "And the peace of God [that peace which reassures the heart, that peace] which transcends all understanding, [that peace which] stands guard over your hearts and your minds in Christ Jesus [is yours]." Satan presents the same issue and does not even bother to redress it, and I repeatedly embrace what God has forgiven. As we read in 1 John 1:9 (AMP), "If we [freely] admit that we have sinned and confess our sins, He is faithful and just [true to His nature and promises] and will forgive our sins and cleanse us continually from all unrighteousness [and wrongdoing, everything not in conformity with His will and purpose]." He cleansed me from all unrighteousness and forgave me, but I walk in condemnation. Do I think I am not worthy of God's grace and mercy and allow myself to receive the guilty charge? I confessed my sin to Jesus, but I continue to be bound by shame.

Let's unpack this. I have been cleansed by God, but the stronghold of condemnation has roots embedded in my soul so deep that I continue to walk in bondage. Bondage is the "servitude or subjugation to a controlling person or force." Have I allowed what a person says or thinks to take priority over what God says? Second Corinthians 10:4–5 (NIV) says, "The weapons we fight with are not the weapons of the world. On the contrary, they have the divine power to demolish strongholds. We demolish arguments and every pretension that sets itself up against the knowledge of God, and we take captive every thought to make it obedient to Christ." I confess that I am cleansed by God and worthy of receiving the cleansing power of the Word and the cleansing power of the Blood of Jesus. Today I repent to You, Father God, and I apologize to myself for allowing Satan the opportunity to try to steal the ability to walk in self-forgiveness. I have allowed him to trigger the strongholds of anger, bitterness, and resentment that have entrenched themselves in my soul. I have received the guilty charge even though God has said not guilty. I see Jesus' Blood. Jesus paid the price that we might be free. He is our sacrificial Lamb of God, who shed His blood for us and redeemed us back to God.

There is no self-forgiveness until I receive that God has forgiven me. The deceitful lies of Satan hold us in condemnation and imprison us by turning the guilty key. However, to remain free, I must embrace the Word of God by faith. Ephesians 4:23 (AMP) says, "Be continually renewed in the spirit of your mind [having a fresh, untarnished mental and spiritual attitude]." He wants us to have a sound mind. The word says that God has not given us the spirit of fear: but of power, love, and a sound mind.

Jesus gave His life for our sins. His grace and mercy have set us free from guilt. Titus 3:5 (KJV) says, "Not by works of righteousness which we have done, but according to His mercy He saved us, by the washing of regeneration, and renewing of the Holy Ghost." His mercy and grace set us free. Deuteronomy 4:31 (KJV) says, "(For the LORD thy God is a merciful God;) He will not forsake thee, neither destroy thee nor forget the covenant of thy fathers which He sware unto them." God's grace is His free and unmerited favor toward us. He has washed and renewed His Holy Spirit in me. The verdict is not guilty. No shame charge for us is in Christ Jesus. Isaiah 61:10 (NKJV) says, "I will greatly rejoice in the LORD, My soul shall be joyful in my God; For He has clothed me with garments of salvation, He has covered me with the robe of righteousness, As a bridegroom decks himself with ornaments, And as a bride adorns herself with jewels".

It was the sin of unforgiveness that birthed the shame. Let's put shame in its place. As we read in Romans 3:23 (KJV), "For we have all sinned and fall short of the glory of God." My ability to release the shame is not always at the level it should be. In the past, I have doubted myself, but now I listen closely to the voice of the Holy Spirit.

I have beaten myself up and struggled to move on. In the pit with the lies of the enemy on continuous replay is a dangerous place to be. Should we not talk to God, seek the Holy Spirit for understanding, and ask what triggered that response or action? Self-forgiveness is a choice. Today, I choose to extend empathy and forgiveness to myself and walk in it. I believe by faith, confidence, and trust in God my struggles are over.

Focus Scripture: Ephesians 4:23 (AMP): "And be continually renewed in the spirit of your mind [having a fresh, untarnished mental and spiritual attitude]."

CHAPTER 6

THE RELEASE

To release means "to allow or enable to escape from confinement; set free, allow to move, act, or flow freely."

I mentioned previously the sixth grader who was spiritually wounded on the playground. I am seventy-three years old, and I have learned that the toxins were deeply rooted in my soul and are still an active part of my life.

In the Women's Ministry, we discussed what makes a person stiffen up when hugged and appear to be socially awkward. I tend to be guarded and have walls around me that keep people out. I have been called stand-offish. The wounded sixth grader is very much a part of me. Pastor Brenda shared with me that the root cause of the issue had to be dealt with, or the behavior would continue to come back. It may lay dormant for a season, but it would resurface again.

I decided that I was tired of going around the mountain of anger, bitterness, resentment, and frustration. I concluded that I needed mental health counseling. I do not like myself when that part of me surfaces. When triggered, she is nasty, cold, and rude.

During counseling, Pastor Brenda guided me through the process. I told her (the sixth grade Florine) spirit she no longer existed. I released her to rest in the hands of Jesus. I wrote her a letter, buried it in a special place, and covered it with a container that contained a rose bush called peace. Some days I must remind myself that she no longer exists. I feel like I am missing someone, but I remind myself, and speak aloud, that she is resting in the hands of Jesus. All is well with my soul.

Again, I journal daily, acknowledging my struggles and my victories. After all, condemnation, guilt, and shame were a part of my life of fifty-nine or sixty years. John 8:36 (KJV) says, "If the Son therefore shall make you free, ye shall be free indeed." The release allows a person to leave the jail, cage, or prison. I have been imprisoned by condemnation, guilt, and shame for the last time. I had forgiven myself on numerous occasions, but I had not been able to stay free from the prison of guilt, shame, and condemnation. They were my constant companions.

I have released her (the sixth-grade Florine) into the hands of Jesus to allow her to rest. This has allowed me to forgive and release myself for the many years that the toxins (bitterness, anger, and resentment) had operated in my life. Yes. They were legal because Jesus had forgiven me. However, because the root cause had not been dealt with, the roots continued to grow deeper, lying dormant and resurfacing when triggered by anger.

Recently, I have noticed calm in my spirit and soul. The things that would have triggered a negative response in the past no longer have that effect on me, and I can respond civilly. I refuse to allow offenses to bind me again and forfeit the peace and calmness in my soul.

I've written a letter to myself acknowledging the victories

that God has won in my life. Jeremiah 29:11 (NIV) says, "For I know the plans I have for you,' declares the Lord, 'plans to prosper you and not to harm you, plans to give you hope and a future.'"

Today I am at peace with God, and myself, and I pray at peace with people. John 14:27 (AMP) says, "Peace I leave with you; My [perfect] peace I give unto you; not as the world gives do give to you. Do not let your heart be troubled, nor let it be afraid. [Let My perfect peace calm you in every circumstance and give you courage and strength for every challenge]."

Focus Scripture: John 14:27 (AMP): "Peace I leave with you; My [perfect] peace I give unto you, not as the world gives do I to you. Do not let not your heart be troubled, nor let it be afraid. [Let My perfect peace calm you in every circumstance and give you courage and strength for every challenge]."

CHAPTER 7

THRIVE IN CHRIST JESUS

There have been days when I have been in constant battle with evil spirits. But the word of God says, "greater is He who is in me than he who is in the world" (1 John 4:4). God said it, I believe it, I receive it, and that settles it in my spirit.

I confess that, indeed, who the Son has set free is free indeed. Galatians 5:1 (NIV) says, "It is for freedom that Christ has set us free. Stand firm, then, and do not let yourselves be burdened again with the yoke of slavery." For many years I have been tormented by the noises of abuse. These were the results of the fist, the slaps, and even a rifle butt to the side of my head.

I thank God that He never stopped loving me and unpacking the trunk of spiritual strongholds, the deceitful lies of the enemy that were operating in my life. These strongholds grew from the years of physical and emotional abuse. I did not talk to Pastor Brenda about the physical and emotional abuse as an adult, but I believe while we talked about the emotional abuse of the sixth-grade Florine, who is now resting in the hands of Jesus. The Holy Spirit ministered to the trauma (the emotional wounds) from the spiritual and mental abuse I had endured. I can't believe I'm writing this, but it is part of preparing the soil for me to thrive and flourish.

There is peace and quietness in my spirit and soul. I do not have the words to express what I'm experiencing this morning, but I thank God and I look forward to seasons of the same inner calmness. By the grace and mercy of God, I have endured more than fifty-nine or sixty years of suffering to get to this season of my life. I hear in my spirit, "Rise and shine." Isaiah 60:1 (AMP) says, "Arise [from spiritual depression to a new life], shine (be radiant with the glory of the LORD); for the light has come, And the glory and brilliance of the LORD have risen upon you." The mental and physical strongholds that Satan devised to destroy me have been destroyed in the name of Jesus.

At the age of seventy-three, I'm excited about flourishing to new levels in Christ Jesus. I can truly say that the unspeakable joy of the Lord is my strength. There is no guilt, no shame, and no condemnation in my soul.

In Denver, our yard was one of the places where I fellowshipped with God. Now I spend more time on the porches and in the yard, back to the places of solace for my spirit and soul. There is an inner peace when I spend time in the garden. Psalm 1:3 (KJV) says, "And he shall be like a tree planted by the rivers of water, that bringeth forth his fruit in his season; his leaf also shall not wither; and whatsoever he doeth shall prosper."

The Spirit of the Lord keeps saying, "Thrive! Thrive! Thrive!" John 10:10 (AMP) says, "The thief comes only to steal and kill and destroy. I came that they may have life, and have it in abundance [to the full, till it overflows]." Thrive and flourish in the courts of the Lord. Psalm 92:13–15 (AMP) says, "Planted in the house of the LORD, They will flourish in the courts of our God. [Growing in grace] they will thrive and bear fruit and prosper in old age; They will flourish and be vital and fresh [rich in trust and love and contentment]." I fret less and think about Jesus more.

The cankerworm and locust have tarnished years of prosperity, but I never lost hope. I look forward to the restoration, and recovering all that God has for Al and me in this season of our lives in the name of Jesus. As we read in Romans 15:13 (AMP), "May the God of hope fill you with all joy and peace in believing [through the experience of your faith] that by the power of the Holy Spirit, you will abound in hope and overflow with confidence in His promise."

Today, the Holy Spirit spoke rest in my spirit, and He reminded me of a visual that Pastor Brenda had ministered to me during counseling. Last night, I was resting in His left hand, and He covered me with His right hand. Rest is required to thrive and flourish in the Lord and the noises were sent to deprive me of sleep. My godson's mother posted on social media, "Did you know that sleep was a gift, and the Bible warns against overworking and not sleeping." Psalm 127:2 (AMP) says, "It is vain for you to rise early, To retire late, To eat of the bread of anxious labors- For He gives [blessings] to His beloved even in his sleep." Is fretting a form of spiritual work in the soul that keeps me from sleeping and resting in the Lord? Forgive me, Lord, for the numerous nights that I lost sleep fretting.

For years, Satan has bombarded me with negative thoughts, words, and images. I was consumed with negative images of my life and inundated with the results of old emotional wounds. He toyed with my soul and filled it with deceitful lies. Today, I declare that the yoke of slavery is no longer on my neck and shoulders or saddled on my back. I will meditate on God's thoughts for me. Jeremiah 29:11 (NIV) says, "⧈ For I know the plans I have for you,' declares the Lord, 'plans to prosper you and not to harm you, plans to give you hope and a future.'"

This is my declaration in the name of Jesus.

I will live by faith in the Son of God who loved me and gave Himself for me.

Galatians 2:20 NIV

His grace and peace have been multiplied unto me.

2 Peter 1:2–3

I'm the righteousness of God in Christ Jesus

2 Corinthians 5:21

I come in agreement with David's prayer and I'm the apple of His eye, cherished and favored by God.

Psalm 17:8

I'm more than a conqueror in Christ

Jesus.Romans 8:37

I'm triumphant in Christ.

2 Corinthians 2:14

I bind the hands of the enemy.
He can no longer illegally operate in our lives, the lives of our family, friends, church, and those He has purposed for me to pray for and minister to in the name of Jesus.

Matthew 16:18

I'm a person who defeats the opposition in my life conflicts and struggles with the Word of God.

1 John 4:4

I will flourish in the courts of our Lord bear fruit in my old age. I will stay fresh and green.

Psalm 92:13–14

I shall not die, but live, and declare the works of the Lord.

Psalm 118:17

Amen, and by faith in the finished work of Jesus, I believe and receive that this is my season to flourish in the plan and purpose that God has for my life.

Focus Scripture: Galatians 5:1 (NIV): "It is for freedom that God has set us free. Stand firm, then, and do not let yourselves be burdened again by the yoke of slavery."

CHAPTER 8

THE POWER TO DEMOLISH STRONGHOLDS

In chapter three, I talked about pulling down strongholds, casting down imaginations, and dressing for spiritual battles. In chapter seven, I wrote about thriving in Christ Jesus. This chapter will allow us to hear what God has to say about specific mental strongholds/spirits. It is not an all-inclusive list of demonic influences that invade our souls, but it will address some of the mental challenges in our lives. I will define/describe how the spirit operates in our souls and give scriptures to address the specific stronghold. The Word declares that they (believers) overcame him (Satan), by the blood of the Lamb (Jesus), and the word of their testimony.

We must remember that demonic influences are spirit, but the Word of God is Spirit. God says in Hebrews 4:12 (KJV), "For the Word of God is quick, and powerful, and sharper than any two-edged sword, piercing even to the dividing asunder of the soul and spirit, and of the joints and marrow, and is a discerner of the thoughts and intents of the heart." Also, the Word of God declares and decrees in Second Corinthians 10:4 (NIV),

"The weapons we fight with are not weapons of the world. On the contrary, they have divine power to demolish strongholds." Our focus must be that Jesus is our stronghold. Psalm 9:9 (KJV) says, "The LORD also will be a refuge for the oppressed, A refuge in times of trouble." Jesus said in Luke 10:19 (AMP), "Listen carefully: I have given you authority [that you now possess] to tread on serpents and scorpions, and [the ability to exercise authority] over all the power of the enemy (Satan), and nothing will [in any way] harm you." Our goal must be to thrive and live the life that God purposed for us to live.

Aligning ourselves with the Word of God is necessary. We do this by renewing our minds daily with the Word of God, speaking the Word with confidence, and having an intimate relationship with Jesus.

Romans 12:2 (NLT) says, "Don't copy the behavior and customs of this world but let God transform you into a new person by changing the way you think. Then you will learn to know God's will for you, which is good and pleasing and perfect." Our souls need to be reprogrammed from the deceitful lies of Satan.

Until we Realize whose we are, and who we are in Christ Jesus, we will continue to embrace the lies and be tormented by the strongholds that have embedded themselves in our spiritual hearts. Jesus is the head of every power and authority and has given us His Word so that we might have a way of escape. Colossians 1:18 (NIV) says, "And He is the head of the body, the church, He is the beginning and the firstborn from among the dead, so that in everything He might have the supremacy." Our thinking must line up with the Word. Philippians 4:8 (KJV) says, "Finally, brethren, whatsoever things are true, whatsoever things are honest, whatsoever things are just, whatsoever things are pure, whatsoever things are lovely, whatsoever things are of a good report; if there be any virtue, and if there be any praise, think on these things."

Earlier, I told you that I am not a psychologist or a psychiatrist. However, I wanted to know how these demonic influences manifested themselves. I desire to be free of these influences and learn how to stay free. Once again, I invite you to go to the study hall with me. The Holy Spirit will lead and guide us all into truth, and reveal the strongholds embedded in our souls. We will study scriptures that will set us free and help to keep us free. As we read in John 8:32 (KJV), "And ye shall know the truth, and the truth shall make you free." The scriptures that we are going to study apply to the saved. As we read in Romans 10:9–10 (AMP),

If you acknowledge and confess with your mouth that Jesus is Lord [recognizing His power, authority, and majesty as God], and believe in your heart that God raised Him from the dead, you will be saved. For with the heart a person believes [in Christ as Savior] resulting in his justification [that is, being made righteous—being freed of the guilt of sin and made acceptable to God]; and with the mouth he acknowledges and confesses [his faith openly], resulting in and confirming [his] salvation. The plan of salvation is simple, and this is how one of the elders at my church ministers it.

A. Admit that you are a sinner.

B. Believe God for who He is.

C. Confess the Lord Jesus Christ.

D. Don't put it off.

PRAYER OF REPENTANCE AND SALVATION

Father God, I admit I am a sinner in need of a Savior. I repent of my sins and invite You into my heart to be my personal Lord and Savior. I believe that Jesus died for my sins and rose from the dead. I am forgiven. I have confessed with my mouth, and I believe with my heart and confess You (Jesus) as my personal Lord and Savior. I believe by faith that I am saved in the name of Jesus. Amen.

If you believe this Word (Romans 10:9–10), receive it into your heart, and confess the above plan of salvation, you are now saved. Welcome to the family of God! At this moment, the Word of God applies to you.

Let's clarify again that "a spiritual stronghold is a habitual pattern of thought, built into one's thought life. Satan and his minions want to capture the minds of people: the mind is the citadel of the soul. He who controls the mind controls a very strategic place."

Psalm 37:39–40 (KJV) says, "But the salvation of the righteous is in the LORD: He is their strength in the time of trouble. And the LORD shall help them, and deliver them: He shall deliver them from the wicked, and save them because they trust Him."

STRONGHOLDS OF THE ENEMY

Below is a list of demonic influences (spirits) that become strongholds in our souls and scriptures (spiritual medicine) to meditate on to help us focus on the Word of God.

DESCRIPTION

A. "The spirit of rejection is an oppressive spirit. It robs you of joy and peace. Oppression is defined as mental pressure or distress. Therefore, if the spirit of rejection is an oppressive spirit, you can think of it as a tactic by the enemy to push or press you down into moods or emotions that block you from experiencing freedom, and the presence of God's love in your life" Curt Landry Ministries, "The Spirit of Rejection."

Satan would have you believe that you are not worthy of God's love. But listen to these scriptures as the Word of God expresses His unconditional love for us.

SPIRITUAL MEDICINE

(1) Psalm 27:10 (AMP): "Although my father and mother have abandoned me, Yet the LORD will take me up [adopt me as His child]." When we receive Jesus as our personal Savior, we become God's children (sons and daughters). We are engrafted into His family (the body of Christ).

(2) John 3:16 (AMP): "For God so [greatly] loved and dearly prized the world, that He [even] gave His [One and] only begotten Son, so that whoever believes and trust in Him

[as Savior] shall not perish, but have eternal life."

(3) Psalm 32:1 (NIV): "Blessed is the one whose transgressions are forgiven, whose sins are covered. Blessed is the one whose sin the LORD does not count against them and in whose spirit is no deceit."

(4) Romans 5:8 (NIV): "But God demonstrates His love for us in this: While we were still sinners, Christ died for us."

While we were wallowing in lustful actions or thoughts, Jesus gave His life for us.

DESCRIPTION

B. The strongholds of fear and worry will grow into anxiety, hopelessness, and despair.

Let's define each of these strongholds.

(1) Fear is "a painful emotion or passion excited by an expectation of evil, or the apprehension of impending danger. Fear expresses less apprehension than dread, and dread less than terror and fright. The force of this passion, beginning with the most moderate degree, may be thus expressed, fear, dread, terror, fright. Fear is accompanied with the desire to avoid or ward off the expected evil. Fear is an uneasiness of mind, upon the thought of future evil likely to befall us."

(2) To display courage "means to stand up despite the world—even if the world is laughing at you, even if the world does not believe you, and even if the world does not want what you want to give it – and explain to the world with love, patience and high spirits what benefits the world, what brings peace to the world and what benefits humanity's salvation

today" Micheal Laitman, "What is Courage".

(3) Worry is "to strangle. Over time it developed to mean to cause mental distress or trouble." Andrew Shykofsky, "The Spiritual Side of Worry."

(4) Anxiety "is a feeling of worry, nervousness or unease about something with an uncertain outcome. Anxiety affects us physically, as well as affects our thoughts and behaviors. Anxiety is a normal response and is required to keep us safe from harm."

(5) Hopelessness "is defined as a feeling or state of despair; lack of hope. It is an emotion that steals your motivation and zest for life. It is often rooted in the desire to place situations and circumstances on your timetable, rather than surrendering situations to God in His perfect timing "Curt Landry Ministries "Breaking Free Form Hopelessness."

(6) Despair "is the complete loss of hope" Compelling Truth, "Mental Health."

Now that we have the definitions, let's look at what the Word of God says about spiritual influences.

SPIRITUAL MEDICINE

(1) 2 Timothy 1:7 (AMP): "For God did not give us a spirit of timidity or cowardice or fear, but [He has given us a spirit] of power and love and sound judgment and personal discipline [abilities that result in a calm, well-balanced mind and self-control]."

(2) Philippians 4:6–7 (NIV): "Do not be anxious about anything, but in every situation, by prayer and petition, with thanksgiving, present your request to God. And the peace of

God, which transcends all understanding, will guard your hearts and minds in Christ Jesus."

(3) Jeremiah 29:11 (KJV): "For I know the thoughts that I think toward you, says the LORD, thoughts of peace and not of evil, to give you an expected end."

(4) 1 Peter 5:7 (KJV): "Casting all your care upon Him; for He careth for you."

DESCRIPTION

C. The stronghold of unforgiveness "is hurt, a person who is deeply hurt. A spirit of unforgiveness goes beyond a temporary unwillingness to forgive. The spirit of unforgiveness is a spiritual acid that eats through the spirit within us. The spirit of unforgiveness is a supernatural cancer that slowly and deliberately eats you up" Stronghold of Unforgiveness, "Healed People."

SPIRITUAL MEDICINE

(1) Mark 11:25–26 (NKJV): "And whenever you stand praying, if you have anything against anyone, forgive him, that your Father in heaven may also forgive you your trespasses. But if you do not forgive, neither will your Father in heaven forgive your trespasses."

(2) 1 Peter 5:7 (KJV): "Casting all your care upon Him, for He careth for you."

(3) Matthew 5:44 (KJV): "But I say unto you, Love your enemies, bless them that curse you, do good to them that hate you, and pray for them which despitefully use you, and

persecute you."

Holding grudges, bitterness, and anger in your heart can block the answers to your prayers. God said forgive!

DESCRIPTION

D. The spirit of disappointment "manifests in the form of worry, rejection, and delay. It makes people rush into decisions and take drastic steps that make them lose hope, lose money, possession, and their partner in marriage. The spirit of disappointment does not allow people to believe in themselves" Evangelist Joshua, "Prayers to break Disappointments."

SPIRITUAL MEDICINE

(1) Isaiah 66:2 (NIV): "Has not My hand made all things, and so they came into being? 'declares the LORD'. These are the ones I look on with favor: those who are humble and contrite in spirit, and who tremble at My Word."

(2) Jeremiah 29:11 (NLT): "For I know the plans that I have for you, 'says the LORD.' They are plans for good and not for disaster, to give you a future and a hope."

(3) John 16:33 (KJV): "These things I have spoken unto you, that in me ye might have peace. In the world ye shall have tribulation: but be of good cheer; I have overcome the world."

DESCRIPTION

E. The spirit of self-hatred is "hatred directed toward oneself rather than toward others: self-hate" Merriam-Webster.

"In short, self-hatred results from not living up to standards either we or others have set for acceptability. In our recognition that we can not be perfect, we may descend into self-hatred" Got Questions.org.

SPIRITUAL MEDICINE

(1) Genesis 1:27 (NKJV): "So God created man in His image; in the image of God He created him; male and female He created them."

(2) Psalm 139:14 (NIV): "I praise You because I am fearfully and wonderfully made; your works are wonderful, I know that full well."

(3) Romans 3:23 (NIV): "For all have sinned and fall short of the glory of God."

DESCRIPTION

F. Suicide is "the act or an instance of taking one's own life voluntarily" Webster Dictionary "Suicide."

Spiritual suicide "means to live life without any inquiry into Spiritual topics, without spending time doing Spiritual activities, and a whole lie is spent in simply taking care of the body and at the end of life quitting the body without any spiritual merits is called a Spiritual Suicide" Quora.

SPIRITUAL MEDICINE

(1) God has created us in His image. Genesis 1:27 (NIV) says, "So God created man in His image, in the image of God

He created them; male and female He created them."

(2) John 10:10 (KJV): "The thief cometh not, but for to steal, and to kill, and to destroy: I come that they might have life and that they might have it more abundantly."

(3) 1 Corinthians 3:16–17 (NKJV): "Do you not know that you are the temple of God and that the Spirit of God dwells in you? 17. If anyone defiles the temple of God, God will destroy him. For the temple of God is holy, which temple you are."

(4) 2 Corinthians 12:9 (AMP): "But He said to me, My grace is sufficient for you [My lovingkindness and My mercy are more than enough—always available—regardless of the situation]; for [My] power is being perfected [and is completed and shows itself most effective] in [your] weakness."

DESCRIPTION

G. "Spiritual struggles in coping represents efforts to protect or transform peoples relationship with whatever they hold sacred, including their connection with God/Higher power. Their spiritual identity, and their connections to a religious community."

"Additionally, we know that people with mental illness can be particularly vulnerable to the negative effects of spiritual struggle, particularly when such struggles are not appropriately addressed in an effective and time-sensitive manner" Jamie Aten "Dealing with Spiritual Struggles."

SPIRITUAL MEDICINE

(1) James 5:16 (AMP): "Therefore, confess your sins to one another [your false steps, your offenses], and pray for one another, that you may be healed and restored. The heartfelt and persistent prayer of a righteous man (believer) can accomplish much [when put into action and made effective by God—it is dynamic and can have tremendous power]."

(2) Matthew 5:28 (KJV): "But I say to you, That whosoever looketh on a woman to lust after her hath committed adultery with her already in his heart." Forgive us Father God in the name of Jesus.

(3) Titus 2:11–12 (NLT): "For the grace of God has been revealed, bringing salvation to all people. And we are instructed to turn from godless living and sinful pleasures."

DESCRIPTION

H. "The sin of pride is a heart that encompasses EVERYTHING we do that does not put God first. The unsaved person lives in this condition perpetually. The saved person struggles with denying SELF, who wants its way all the time" Serious Faith.com.

"The sin of pride is a heart attitude expressed in an unhealthy, exaggerated attention to self and elevated view of one's abilities, accomplishments, position, or possessions. Pride has been called "the cancer of the soul, "the beginning of all sin," and "sin in its final form" Mary Fairchild " According to sin in the Bible."

SPIRITUAL MEDICINE

(1) James 4:8 (NIV): "Come near to God and he will come

near to you. Wash your hands, you sinners, and purify your hearts, you double-minded."

(2) Proverb 11:2 (KJV): "When pride cometh, then cometh shame: but with the lowly is wisdom."

(3) 1 Corinthians 13:4 (NIV): "Love is patient, love is kind, it does not envy, it does not boast, it is not proud."

(4) James 4:10 (NIV): "Humbles yourselves before the Lord, and he will lift you ".

(6) 1 Peter 5:5 (KJV): "Likewise, ye younger, submit yourselves unto the elder. Yea, all of you be subject to one another, and be clothed with humility: for God resisteth the proud, and giveth grace to the humble."

DESCRIPTION

I. Mean-spirited "means feeling or showing a cruel desire to cause pain or harm" Webster Dictionary.

SPIRITUAL MEDICINE

(1) Luke 6:28 (NIV) "Bless those who curse you, pray for those who mistreat you."

(2) 1 Corinthians 2:16 (KJV) " For who hath known the mind of the Lord, that he may instruct? But we have the mind of Christ."

(3) Romans 7: 20-22 (AMP)" Now if I do not desire to do, it is no longer I doing it [it is not myself that acts], but the sin [principle] which dwells within me [fixed and operating in my

soul]. 21 So I find it to be a law (rule of action of my being) that when I want to do what is right and good, evil is ever present with me and I am subject to its insistent demands."

(4) Romans 12:2 (NIV) " Do not be conformed to the pattern of this world, but be transformed by the renewing of your mind. Then you will be able to test and approve what God's will is -his good, pleasing, and perfect will."

DESCRIPTION

J. "A religious spirit is a type of demonic spirit that influences a person, or group of people, to replace a genuine relationship with God with works and traditions. When people operate out of a religious spirit they attempt to earn salvation" Curt Landry Ministries, "What is a Religious Spirit?"

SPIRITUAL MEDICINE

(1) James 1:26–27 (NIV): "Those who consider themselves religious and yet do not keep a tight rein on their tongues deceive themselves, and their religion is worthless. 27 Religion that God our Father accepts as pure and faultless is this: to look after orphans and widows in their distress and to keep oneself from being polluted by the world."

(2) Hebrews 12:2 (NIV): "Fixing our eyes on Jesus, the pioneer and perfecter of faith. For the joy set before Him endured the cross, scorning its shame, and sat down at the right hand of the throne of God."

(3) Hebrews 13:20–21 (NKJV): "Now may the God of peace who brought up our Lord Jesus from the dead, that great Shepherd of the sheep, through the blood of the everlasting

covenant, make you complete in every good work to do His will, working in you what is well pleasing in His sight, through Jesus Christ, to whom be glory forever and ever. Amen."

(4) Galatians 5:1 (NIV): "It is for freedom that Christ has set us free. Stand firm, then, and do not let yourselves be burdened again by a yoke of slavery."

DESCRIPTION

K. Spiritual depression "is a loss of spiritual vitality and joy. In terms of Christianity, experiencing a spiritual depression might involve losing touch with your faith " forgetting God, or struggling to find time for spiritual study" Crystal Raypole, "Understanding Spiritual Depression."

SPIRITUAL MEDICINE

(1) Joshua 1:8 (NIV): "Keep this Book of the Law always on your lips; meditate on it day and night, so that you may be careful to do everything written in it. Then you will be prosperous."

(2) Psalm 19:14 (KJV): "Let the words of my mouth, and the meditation of my heart, be acceptable in thy sight, O Lord my strength, and my redeemer."

(3) 1 Peter 2:24–25 (NKJV): "Who Himself bore our sins in His own body on the tree, that we, having died to sins, might live for righteousness—by whose stripes you were healed. For you were like sheep going astray, but have now returned to the Shepherd and Overseer of your souls."

(4) Romans 14:17 (KJV): "For the kingdom of God is not meat and drink, but righteousness, and peace, and joy in the Holy Ghost."

DESCRIPTION

L. "The spirit of frustration is very persistent, aggressive, and determined. When this spirit is programmed in the life of any individual it is catastrophe and chaos mingled with depression which can lead to suicide, heart failure, or heart attack. Many Christians and non-Christians battle with this vicious spirit and have even died from it" Melesia Fisher-Mowatt.

"What is frustration? The definition of frustration is the feeling of being upset, or annoyed, especially because of inability to change or achieve something. Frustration comes when we feel that we don't live up to our potential or standards. We tend to compare ourselves with others and not focus on ourselves. It is born out of resentment, disappointment, pride, envy, anger and rage."

SPIRITUAL MEDICINE

(1) Isaiah 41:10 (AMP): "Do not fear [anything], for I am with you; Do not be afraid, for I am your God. I will strengthen you, be assured I will help you; I will certainly take hold of you with My righteous right hand [a hand of justice, of power, of victory, of salvation]."

(2) 1 Thessalonians 5:18 (AMP): "In every situation [no matter what the circumstances] be thankful and continually give thanks to God; for this is the will of God for you in Christ Jesus."

(3) Colossians 3:8 (NIV): "But now you must also rid

yourselves of all such things as these: anger rage malice, slander, and filthy language from your lips."

DESCRIPTION

M. Self-doubt is a "lack of faith in oneself: a feeling of doubt or uncertainty about one's abilities, actions, etc." Webster Dictionary.

"Doubt in the scripture can be seen to be characteristic of both believers and unbelievers. In believers it is usually a weakness of faith a wavering of in the face of God's promises. In the unbeliever doubt is virtually synonymous with unbelief. Scripture, as would be expected, does not look at doubt philosophically or epistemologically. Doubt is viewed practically and spiritually as it relates to our trust in the Lord For this reason, doubt is not deemed as valuable or commendable."

SPIRITUAL MEDICINE

(1) Philippians 4:13 (KJV): "I can do all things through Christ, which strengthens me."

(2) 2 Timothy 1:7 (KJV): "For God has not given us a spirit of fear; but of power, and love, and a sound mind."

(3) 1 John 4:4 (KJV): "Ye are of God, little children, and have overcome them: because greater is He that is in you, than He that is in the world."

DESCRIPTION

N. Self-esteem "People with overly high self-esteem are often arrogant and self-indulgent and express feelings of entitlement.

They tend to overlook their flaws and criticize others. Low self-esteem: Feeling inferior to others. People with low -self-esteem value the opinions of others above their own." Audrey Sherman, "Characteristics of High and Low Self-Esteem."

(1) Genesis 1:27 (NKJV): "So God created man in His image; in the image of God He him; male and female created He them."

(2) Isaiah 49:16 (NIV): "See, I have engraved you in the palms of my hands; your walls are ever before me."

(3) Psalm 139:14 (NIV): "I praise You because I am fearfully and wonderfully made; your works are wonderful, I know that full well."

Wow! There is a lot to learn about our spiritual make-up. I pray that these descriptions and scriptures will help us to:

- Become better rooted and grounded in the Word of God; and

- Understand the strongholds that are operating in our lives.

Remember that God's love is unconditional, and His heart has no remorse for loving us. He loves us! Let's make it personal. God loves me! He knows the demonic influences and mental challenges that are operating in our lives, but He is waiting for us to invite Him into our spiritual wounds.

Focus Scripture: Hebrews 4:12 (KJV): "For the Word of God is quick, and powerful, and sharper than any twoedge sword, piercing even to the dividing asunder of soul and spirit, and of the joints and marrow, and is a discerner of the thought and intents of the heart."

Thank you for attending the study hall with me. My prayer is that, as we studied, we learned, and we grew in the Word of God. As we read in 2 Timothy 2:15 (NIV), "Do your best to present yourself to God as one approved, a worker who does not need to be ashamed and who correctly handles the word of truth."

PRAYER

Father God, in the name of Jesus, I thank you for Your Word, and the anointing that is on Your Word to break yokes. Your word says to come boldly before Your throne of grace. Father, I come asking You to deliver me from all evil, for thine is the kingdom, the power, and the glory. Father God, Your Word said to be specific when I pray. (Name the stronghold/spirit that you are asking God to deliver you from. Ask for forgiveness for any sin that you may have committed.) I plead the blood of Jesus over the doorpost of my soul. Your Word says that if I confess my sins, Jesus will forgive me and cleanse me from all unrighteousness. I ask You to forgive me of my sins (name them). I declare that by Jesus's stripes, I am healed, and by the blood of Jesus I am delivered from (say what you want to be healed/delivered from). No weapon formed against me shall prosper. I bind the hands of the enemy, and I thank You for manifested answers to my prayers.

I would like to encourage you to pray to God as only you can. Talk to Him about your heartbreaks, disappointments, and frustrations. And if you will listen, He will speak back. First Kings 19:12 (KJV) says, "And after the earthquake a fire; but the LORD was not in the fire: and after the fire, a still small voice."

I wrote this book to help others who have gone or are going through periods of oppression and depression. I hope the experiences and solutions that I have shared will help you.

Thank you and may the blessings of God be manifested in your lives.

NOTES

NOTES

NOTES

ABOUT THE AUTHOR

She is an ordained minister whose vision is to teach the Word of God with understanding and revelation under the anointing of the Holy Spirit, as exemplified in the scripture "…. a teacher of the Gentiles in [the realm of] faith and truth" 1 Timothy 2:7 Amp.

She received Jesus as her personal Savior while serving in the United States Army in Landstuhl, Germany. She joined Rheinland Baptist Church and served in the Children's Church.

Her educational summary includes Aurora Community College, Heritage Bible College, Colorado Christian University, and Survine Bible College, all located in the Denver, Colorado, Area. She earned degrees in Health Care Administration, A Bachelor of Science in Organization Management, and a Master's Degree in Biblical Studies.

Florine was licensed into the ministry in 1991 and ordained in 1995 by Reverend Paul Williams under the Direction of Pastor Donald R. Batson, Sr.

She is a Retired Army, Sergent First Class, and a Disabled Veteran. Also, Florine is a two-time cancer survivor.

Currently, she serves as the Coordinator for Follow Up, connecting with First Time Visitors and New Believers. Also, she is a volunteer teacher in the Children's Church at Christ Worship Center Church, Hope Mills, North Carolina, under Pastor Ricky Harrell Sr. and Co-pastor Dr. Brenda Harrell.

She and her husband (Albert), cover, and friend live in Raeford, North Carolina.

BIBLIOGRAPHY

Page No.

5- Rejection, Good Therapy.Org, "Rejection" https: www. goodtherapy.org/learn-about-therapy /issues/rejection

10- "Imagination" Merriam- Webster.com https://www. merriam-webster.com/dictionary /imagination

13- "Prowl" Merriam–Webster.com https://www. Merriam-webster.com/dictionary /prowl

17- "Toxin" Labroots.com https://www.labroots.com/tag/toxins

17- "Poison" KJV Dictionary https://av1611.com/kjbp/kjv-dictionary/poison .html

17- "Demonic Influences" https://www.gotquestions.org/ demonic-oppression .html

36- "Release" https:// www. Merriam-webster.com/dictionary/ release

33- "Bondage" Merriam-Webster https://www.merriam-webster.com/dictionary/bondage

47- "Pulling Down Strongholds" https:// www.google.com/search?q=definition +fo+a+spiritual+stronghold&oq=definition+ fo+a+spiritual+stronghold&gs_lcrp=EgZjaHJ

vbWUyBggAEEUY...

48- "The Spirit of Rejection" Curt Landry Ministries https://. curtlandry.com.battle-the- spirit-of-rejection/

49- "Fear" KJV Dictionary https://av1611.com/ kjbp/kjv-dictionary/fear.html

49- "What is courage" Quora 1 Michael Laitman https:// whatsbeinghuman.quora.com/ What-is-courage

50- "The Spiritual Side of Worry" Andrew Shykofsky https:// www.meditatecenter.com/spiritual- side-worrying/

50- "What is Anxiety? People Sense https//www.peoplesense. com.au>resource- centre>anxiety

50- "Hopelessness" Curt Landry Ministries https://www. curtlandry.com/vrp2020-break-free- from-hoplessness

50- "Despair" Oxford Dictionaryhttps://oxforddictionary despair

51-"The Stronghold of Unforgiveness"https://www.google.com/ search?searchq=define+th+=stronghold+of+unforgiveness&oq =define+the+stronghold+of+unforgiveness&gs_ lcrp=EgZjaHJvbWUy...

52- "The spirit of Disappointment" Evangelist Joshua.com https://evangelistjoshua. com/break-disappointment/

52- "The spirit of self- hatred" Merriam- Webster https::// www.google.comsearch?q=definition+of+self+hatred+ merriam-webster+dictionary&sca_esv=82300cf3937c 2883&sxsrf=ACQVn09yMRy2XR...

53-Suicidedefinitionhttps://WWW.

google.com/search?q=define+suicide
&oq=define+suicide&gs_lcrp=EgZjaHJvbWU
YBggAEEUYOTIHCAEQABiABDIHCAI
QABiABDIHCA...

53- "What is Spiritual Suicide?" https://www. .quora.com/
What-is-a-spiritual suicide

53- "Spiritual Struggles in Coping with Martial Problems:
Having Spiritual Conflict with God Self, and Others" BGSU ,
https://www.bgsu.edu/arts-and-sciences/ psychology/graduate-
program/clinical/the-   psychology-of-spirituality-and-family/
research-findings/marriage-co...

54- "Dealing with Spiritual Struggles" Jamie Aten https://www.
psychologytoday.com/us/blog/hope-resilience/202006/dealing-
spiritual -struggles

55- "The Sin of Pride" Serious Faith.com https://www.google.
com/search?sca_esv=736f63000bad8be2&sxsrf=ACQVn0-
vRuKPxeZ2DmOuEzG5bNzdG6Zqgg:
1707424169114&q=Proud+heart

55 "The Sin of Pride" According to the Bible Mary Fairchild
https://www.learnreligions.com/the-sin-of-pride-according-to-
the-bible-5080290

56- "Mean- Spirited" Merriam – Webster https://www.merriam-
webster.com/dictionary/mean-spirited#:-text=%3Aexhibiting
or Characterized by meanness, noun

57- "A Religious Spirit" Curt Landry Ministries, https://www.
curtlandry.com/what-is- a-religious-spirit/

58- "Understanding Spiritual Depression" https://www.
healthline.com/health/depression/spiritual-depression

59- "The Spirit of Frustration" divinetransformation.net https://www.divinetransformation.net/the-spirit-of-frustration/

59- "What is Frustration" https://chosenbyhisgrace.com/spirit-of-frustration/

60-"Self-doubt"Merriam-Websterhttps://www.google.com/searchQ=merriam-webster.com%2Fdictionary%2Fdictionary&2self+self-doubt&oq=merriam-webster.com%2Fself+doubt&g...

60 "Doubt in the Scripture" Baker Evangelical Dictionary of Bible Theology, http://www.biblestudytools.com/dictionaries/bakers-evangelical-dictionary/doubt.html

60-"Self-esteem"HighandLowself–esteem, AudreyShermanpage1https:www.google.com/search?q=define+high+and+low+self+esteem+audrey+sherm+an&oq=define+high+low+self+audrey+sherman&...